I AM A VETERAN

An illustrated poem by
ANDREA CHRISTENSEN BRETT

Text and illustrations © 2017 Andrea Christensen Brett ★ All rights reserved. No part of this publication may be reproduced, stored in a retrieval system, or transmitted in any form by any means, electronic, mechanical, photocopy, recording, or otherwise, without the prior permission of the publisher, except as provided by USA copyright law. ★ Published by TAB Creative, Branson, Missouri ★ Printed in the United States of America by R.C. Brayshaw & Company, Warner, New Hampshire ★ Cover and book design by Melissa Luangrath ★ ISBN: 978-0-692-92582-9 ★ Library of Congress: 2017911778 ★ Visit iamaveteran.net to learn more about this book and the I Am a Veteran Project.

ACKNOWLEDGEMENTS

I am very grateful for the many people who assisted in the creation of this book, who contributed in ways large and small, seen and unseen. I would like to especially acknowledge a few:

My husband, Tom, for his patience with my creative process and his willingness to do the tedious, thankless tasks that are always necessary for an undertaking like this. His love, time, and hard work are in every page.

My children, Briahna, Brydon, and Garon for being my most avid cheerleaders and encouraging my vision. They are my *magnum opus* and my biggest inspiration for any of my other creative works such as this.

My grandsons, Ivan, Auggie, and Wade, who, at the time of this writing await the safe return of their Daddy, TSgt Merrill Perkins, who is deployed with the US Air Force in the Middle Eastern desert. I have held back tears during their sweet prayers and have loved being part of their "home fires burning" team. Because of them and our brave daughter, this project took on even deeper meaning.

Saul Rip Hansen, for joining me in this endeavor which turned out to be much bigger than either of us imagined. Thankfully, he shares my DNA and empathizes with my perfectionistic ways. I appreciate his willingness to work day and night to coordinate the artistic team, and to put his own pencil into action.

The amazing artists: Elizabeth Moug, Brian Astle, Brittany Gneiting, Karen Neil, Chris Holquist, Blake Davis, Gavin Boothe, Melissa Luangrath, and, of course, Saul. If I could not be blessed with their artistic talents, I'm certainly glad they were! I'm so grateful they somehow found the extra hours to help create this beautiful collection of art and design.

Brenda Meadows (SGT, US Army) for her time, her advice, her encouragement, and her beautiful photos.

All my friends of Vietnam Veterans of America, Chapter 913, in Branson, Missouri, who have been ever present in my mind throughout the creation of this book. These men and women hold a very special place in my heart.

My Heavenly Father — my *Sine Qua Non,* and Author of everything good in my life. I humbly acknowledge the many miracles that have attended this offering from first inspiration to gratifying fruition. He has again and again proved His love for me and for His veterans. ✶

ABOUT THE POEM

Many years ago, on a sunny Veteran's Day morning, in McKinney, Texas, I was listening to the radio and heard the local DJ recite a beautiful poem dedicated to our nation's military veterans. I was very moved by it. In fact, it brought me to tears. I wasn't raised in a military family, but something about this poem struck me at the heart and stirred in me an appreciation and awareness I hadn't felt before. I wanted to get a copy of it, but there was no mention of the name of the author. I intended to call the station to inquire as to its source, but the day got away from me and I never did.

Two years later, through a series of providential events, our family began an exciting and terrifying new adventure. We left our home in Texas to start our own musical variety show in Branson, Missouri. We soon learned that part of what makes Branson so unique is its long-held tradition of honoring God, family, and country and the way the town takes special care of veterans. Every show in Branson had a tribute to veterans, and we included one in ours as well. As time went on, we decided we wanted to change our presentation and offer something that could not be heard in any of the other theaters. We wanted to write our own patriotic music and use content that was unique to us. That's when I remembered the poem I had heard back in Texas. I immediately phoned the radio station to track it down to use in our show. I spoke with the programmer who did a thorough search. I was very disappointed when no one at the station could recall what I was talking about. I was puzzled and thought that maybe I was calling the wrong station, so I started calling others. No one I spoke with had any recollection of this poem. I started to wonder if I had really even heard it! I finally gave up on making calls, but was determined to find it elsewhere — I just knew it would be perfect for our tribute.

Then one day, an unexpected thought popped into my head, "You can write your own poem." I dismissed the idea at first, but the inspiration gradually began to take hold. I started thinking of all the veterans I had met and spoken with at our show. They were all just average looking folks, but they told amazing stories of sacrifice and service. For several months, their stories ran around in my head. Then those stories began to line up, and then they began to rhyme. Finally one morning, I said to my family, "I need some time to myself — no distractions, no interruptions, please. I've got a poem I need to write." I locked myself in my basement office, and with a prayer, I began. That was a sacred day for me as I sat at my computer and worked through a flow of inspiration. I felt the touch of the Divine and have never felt that the poem is really my own. I refined it over the next few weeks, then memorized it for our show. It was graciously received, and I've been reciting it ever since.

So, the poem, *I Am a Veteran*, was inspired by "average" men and women. When they are not wearing a uniform to distinguish them from everyone else in the crowd, they look just like you and me. They come in all shapes, sizes, colors, ages, and backgrounds, yet they share one very important bond — military service to the greatest country on earth. On each of their faces and in each of their hearts is a story that may never be told, and even for those stories that are, words in any language are not sufficient to fully capture what happened. Many believe their story isn't worth telling, that their contribution was small and just part of their duty. Many of their stories are too painful to tell. Many don't share because no one has asked them to. In any case, it is these individual experiences that combine together to create a mighty force for freedom. These stories make up the bigger story of America—a story of courage, sacrifice, faith, honor, love, and commitment to preserve and protect her precious liberties.

I wrote *I Am a Veteran* to pay tribute to those who lived this story. Each line or phrase in the poem is the voice of one of these men or women. Each represents an actual person that I have met or have been told about. The poem is not about one veteran, but each and all.

Since it is impossible to cover the scope of their diverse experiences, the words are intended more to be a symbol of the soldier's sacrifice. My hope has always been that each veteran who reads this poem will find themselves somewhere in it and feel acknowledged, honored and appreciated.

I also wrote the poem for those who read or hear it to become more aware of the men and women they encounter in their everyday comings and goings. Maybe he or she is a veteran. Maybe we should ask, "Has he or she had a part in securing MY freedom? Has this 'common' looking person performed uncommon service on MY behalf?" If so, the ground we share in our daily walk is truly sacred ground.

I have now recited this poem thousands of times in our show in Branson and in venues all across the country. I have been amazed and humbled to hear of the places it has been read and used by others — at military funerals, Sunday church services, patriotic memorials, school assemblies, on monuments, on living room walls, in scrapbooks. The poem has opened doors for me and my family to rub shoulders with some of the finest people on earth. I have been told by many veterans that my poem has given them a voice. This is the highest compliment I could possibly receive. It is truly an honor to think I could ever speak for any of these noble men and women who have given so much. It is with deepest gratitude that I offer *I Am a Veteran* as my gift to these great Americans. ★

ABOUT THE BOOK

Not long after writing *I Am a Veteran*, I began to feel the need and desire to put it into book form. I talked about it for many years and knew I would not feel settled in my heart until it was done. But with the demands of a very busy and full life, years came and went, each leaving me with that lingering, nagging feeling. At the end of 2016, for a variety of reasons, our family decided to make a big change in our typical Branson show schedule for the year 2017. This opened a narrow window of time, and I knew it was now, or most likely, never. I sat down with my family to get their thoughts and ideas. Their input encouraged me and increased my vision and, finally, I set out to make the *I Am a Veteran* book a reality.

From the beginning, when I imagined this book, I pictured it with actual photographs that represented each line of the poem. Years ago, I even began collecting photos from some of the veterans who came to our show. For a long time, those photos sat in a filing cabinet drawer. When I began the book project in earnest, I went back into that drawer and looked at them again. Though I loved the photos, I began to feel unsettled about this approach. It was right around that time that I had a random and fortuitous phone conversation with my nephew, Saul Rip Hansen. Saul is an author, an architect, and one of the most gifted artists I have personally known. It's important to note that though I have always had tremendous love and respect for Saul, our paths rarely cross, and this conversation was the first we had in a very long time. We talked at length about his writing and an exciting creative project he was involved with. Speaking with Saul is always inspiring, and this was an energizing conversation for me. Just as it was about to close, I felt the nudge to ask him if I could run an idea by him. I told him about my book project — the poem and the photos. Then he said the magic words — "Aunt Andrea, have you considered pencil drawings?" Though I personally cannot draw a stick figure, I have always been deeply affected by great art, and I immediately knew this was the direction to go. This led to many further conversations with Saul and my husband, Tom, to create a shared vision and to put together a plan to bring it about. Saul used his associations in the world of visual arts to assemble a team of extremely talented artists and designers, each with their own unique style, to bring the poem to life.

My role in the artistic aspect of this book was to select photographs for the artists to use as inspiration for their drawings. It seemed this would be simple enough, but I soon realized that it was much harder than I thought to find photos that fit my criteria. My desire was to find compelling images to represent the different military branches and war eras and to depict diversity in age, gender, and race. At the same time, the pictures needed to lend themselves to being drawn with a pencil. Each piece not only needed to be able to stand on its own in beauty and interest, but also combine with the others to create an inspiring collective gallery. In this pursuit, I have spent countless hours looking at thousands of images. Over the months spent at my computer immersed in military photographs, I have seen images of courage, pain, compassion, strength, despair, pride, and fellowship. At times, it overwhelmed me. I have cried, I have laughed, I have sighed, I have gasped, and I've realized that there is no way for me or for anyone who hasn't lived it to know the heart of a soldier and what it actually means to be a veteran. This process was very important for me because it gave me an even stronger desire to make this book something truly special. The ultimate goal of the entire *I Am a Veteran* team has been to create a work that is completely worthy of its subject.

I also have a larger vision for this book. My desire is for it to be used as a tool to come to know and appreciate our veterans better. I envision older veterans with grandchildren in their laps, turning pages and saying, "This reminds me of when…" I see veterans of all ages, when and if the right time comes, starting a dialogue with their families and friends about their experiences. I would love for this book to be a gentle catalyst for opening those discussions so their legacy can live on to future generations.

But the book is not just for veterans. I would love to see it in homes, in classrooms, in waiting rooms, in libraries, and in churches — increasing awareness in all Americans of the real people behind their freedoms. Because so much of what is in the veteran's heart is unknown, I believe that, as a society, we need to learn more, so their service and sacrifice is not taken for granted. I also care deeply about the patriotic pulse of America, and I would feel supremely honored if this book, in some small way, could engender feelings of greater patriotism, and help those who read it feel deeper love for and devotion to the United States of America.

In the end, however, the book is a fulfillment of an inward commission and a way for me to express my personal gratitude for those who have served or will serve in a military uniform. I do not pretend to know or understand what they have been through—that is known only to them and the Creator of earth and heaven. But I do understand that it is to this Divine Partnership—soldier and Savior—that I owe my freedom. And I am forever grateful. ✶

*To the men and women of the Armed Forces of
the United States of America, past, present, and future.
Thank you for defending and protecting freedom
all around the world.*

I AM A VETERAN

An illustrated poem by
ANDREA CHRISTENSEN BRETT

You may not know me
    the first time we meet
I'm just another
    you see on the street

But I am the reason
you walk and breathe free
I am the reason
for your liberty

I am a veteran

I work in the local factory all day
    I own the restaurant just down the way

I sell you insurance, I start your IV

I've got the best looking grandkids you'll ever see

I'm your grocer, your banker
Your child's school teacher

I'm your plumber, your barber
Your family's preacher

But there's part of me
    you don't know very well
Just listen a moment
    I've a story to tell

I am a veteran

I joined the service
while still in my teens

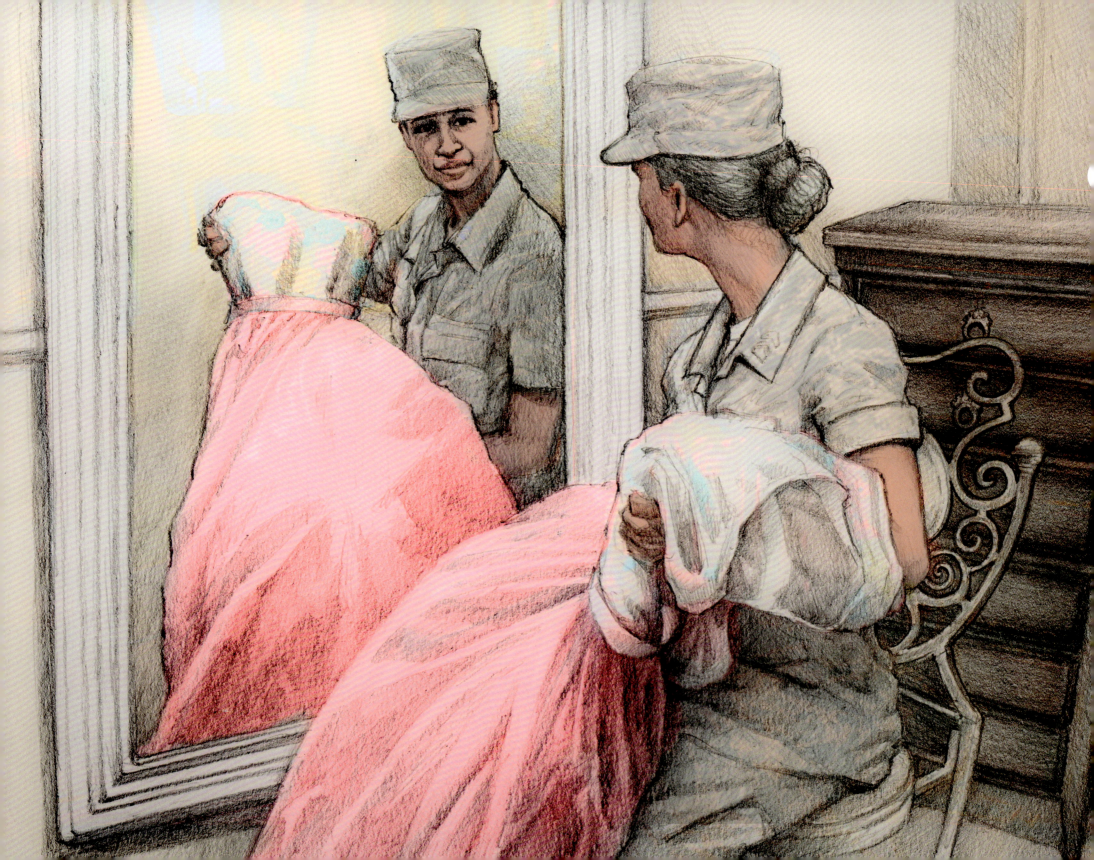

I traded my prom dress
    for camouflage greens

I'm the first in my family
    to do something like this

I followed my father
    like he followed his

Defying my fears and hiding my doubt
    I married my sweetheart before I shipped out

I missed Christmas, then Easter, the birth of my son
But I knew I was doing what had to be done

I served on the battlefront

I served on the base

I bound up the wounded
 and begged for God's grace

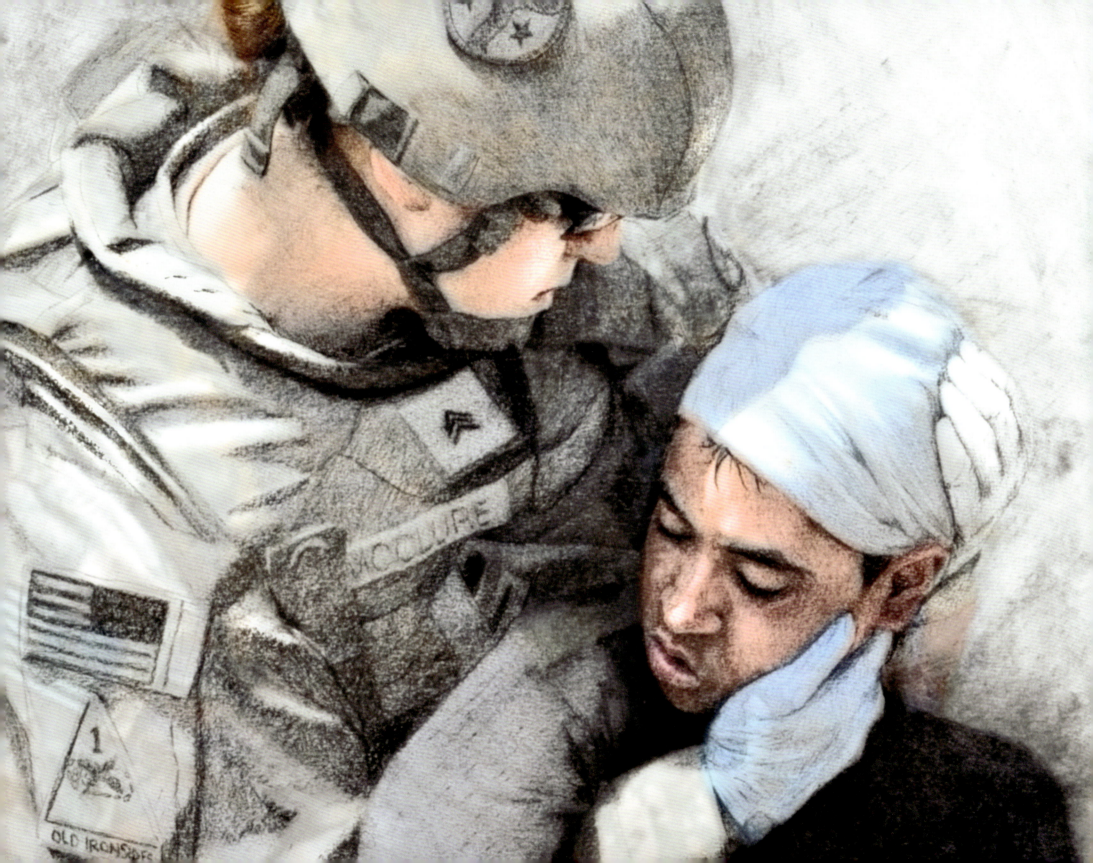

I gave orders to fire

I followed commands

I marched into conflict
   in far distant lands

In the jungle

the desert

on mountains

and shores

In bunkers, in tents, on dank earthen floors

While I fought on the ground

in the air

on the sea

—My family and friends
    were home praying for me

For the land of the free and the home of the brave
I faced my demons in foxholes and caves

Then one dreaded day without drummer or fife
I lost an arm, my buddy lost his life

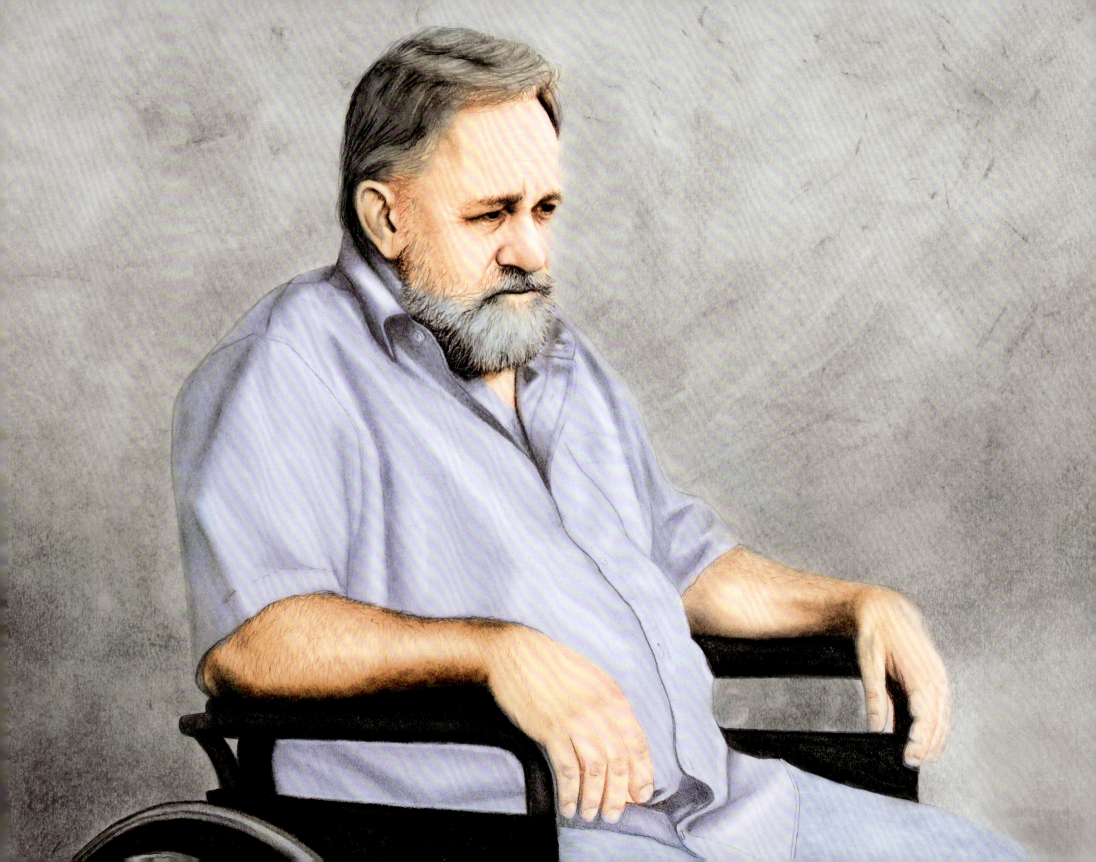

I came home and moved on but forever was changed
The perils of war in my memory remained

I don't really say much, I don't feel like I can
But I left home a child and came home a man

There are thousands like me
      Thousands more who are gone
But their legacy lives as time marches on

White crosses in rows

And names carved in queue
Remind us of what these brave souls had to do

I'm part of a fellowship

A strong, mighty band

of each man and each woman
    who has served this great land

And when Old Glory waves
    I stand proud, I stand tall

I helped keep her flying
Over you, over all

I AM A VETERAN

I AM A VETERAN

by Andrea Christensen Brett

You may not know me the first time we meet

I'm just another you see on the street

But I am the reason you walk and breathe free

I am the reason for your liberty

I AM A VETERAN

I work in the local factory all day

I own the restaurant just down the way

I sell you insurance, I start your IV

I've got the best-looking grandkids you'll ever see

I'm your grocer, your banker

Your child's schoolteacher

I'm your plumber, your barber

Your family's preacher

But there's part of me you don't know very well

Just listen a moment, I've a story to tell

I AM A VETERAN

I joined the service while still in my teens

I traded my prom dress for camouflage greens

I'm the first in my family to do something like this

I followed my father, like he followed his

Defying my fears and hiding my doubt

I married my sweetheart before I shipped out

I missed Christmas, then Easter, the birth of my son

But I knew I was doing what had to be done

I served on the battlefront, I served on the base

I bound up the wounded and begged for God's grace

I gave orders to fire, I followed commands

I marched into conflict in far distant lands

In the jungle, the desert, on mountains, and shores

In bunkers, in tents, on dank earthen floors

While I fought on the ground, in the air, on the sea

My family and friends were home praying for me

For the land of the free and the home of the brave
I faced my demons in foxholes and caves
Then one dreaded day, without drummer or fife
I lost an arm, my buddy lost his life

I came home and moved on, but forever was changed
The perils of war in my memory remained
I don't really say much, I don't feel like I can
But I left home a child, and came home a man

There are thousands like me, thousands more who are gone
But their legacy lives as time marches on
White crosses in rows and names carved in queue
Remind us of what these brave souls had to do

I'm part of a fellowship, a strong mighty band
Of each man and each woman who has served this great land
And when Old Glory waves, I stand proud, I stand tall
I helped keep her flying over you, over all

I AM A VETERAN

ARTISTS & ATTRIBUTIONS

The illustrations in *I Am a Veteran* were inspired by actual photographs & hand drawn by gifted artists.

"You may not know me"
Artist: Saul Rip Hansen
Photo courtesy Sheila Smart Photography

"I own the restaurant"
Artist: Brittany Gneiting
Photo courtesy Meadows Images, Branson, MO

"Your child's school teacher"
Artist: Blake Davis
Photo courtesy 123RF
Photographer: Cathy Yeulet

"I am the reason"
Artist: Blake Davis
Photographer: Briahna Brett Perkins

"I start your IV"
Artist: Blake Davis
Photo courtesy iStock
Photographer: Monkey Business Images

"Your family's preacher"
Artist: Elizabeth Moug
Photo courtesy Getty Images
Photographer: Jeremy Woodhouse

"I am a veteran-WWII"
Artist: Elizabeth Moug
Photo courtesy Freethink Media

"I've got the best looking grandkids"
Artist: Saul Rip Hansen
Photographer: Jenna Reyna

"Just listen a moment, I've a story to tell"
Artist: Saul Rip Hansen
Photo courtesy Meadows Images, Branson, MO

"I am a veteran-young woman"
Artist: Brittany Gneiting
Photo courtesy Meadows Images, Branson, MO

"Still in my teens"
Artist: Karen Neil
Photo courtesy Meadows Images, Branson, MO

"I traded my prom dress"
Artist: Blake Davis
Photo courtesy Meadows Images, Branson, MO

"I'm the first in my family"
Artist: Elizabeth Moug
Photographer: Unknown

"I followed my father"
Artist: Blake Davis
Photographer: Andrea C. Brett

"I married my sweetheart"
Artist: Brian Astle
Copyright Kevin Millard, KMI Photography Inc.

"The birth of my son"
Artist: Elizabeth Moug
Photo courtesy US Marine Corps
Photographer: Lance Cpl. Matthew Manning

"On the battlefront"
Artist: Brian Astle
Photo courtesy U.S. Army
Photographer: Spc. 5th Class John Olsen

"On the base"
Artist: Blake Davis
Photo courtesy US Air Force
Photographer: Master Sgt. Jack Braden

"I bound up the wounded"
Artist: Brittany Gneiting
Photo courtesy US Army
Photographer: Sgt. Michael Carden

"I gave orders to fire"
Artist: Brian Astle
Photo courtesy US Air Force
Photographer: Senior Airman Christopher Gross

"I followed commands"
Artist: Blake Davis
Photo courtesy US Marine Corp
Photographer: Petty Officer 3rd Class Jeannette Mullinax

"I marched into conflict"
Artist: Elizabeth Moug
Photo courtesy US Air Force
Photographer: Staff Sgt. Ryan Crane

"In the jungle"
Artist: Elizabeth Moug
Photo courtesy US Air Force
Photographer: Staff Sgt. Ryan Crane

"The desert"
Artist: Brittany Gneiting
Photo courtesy US Air Force
Photographer: Senior Airman Krystal Ardrey

"On mountains"
Artist: Blake Davis
Composite photos courtesy Program Exec. Office
Soldier & US Army 10th Mtn. Division

"On shores"
Artist: Blake Davis
Photo courtesy US Army
165th Signal Combat Camera Co.
Photographer: Pvt. Louis Weintraub

"On dank earthen floors"
Artist: Brian Astle
Photo courtesy US Marine Corps
Photographer: Cpl. Aaron S. Patterson

"On the ground"
Artist: Brittany Gneiting
Photo courtesy US Navy
Photographer: Petty Officer 2nd Class
Joan E. Kretschmer

"In the air"
Artist: Saul Rip Hansen
Photo courtesy US Air Force
Photographer: Airman 1st Class
Trevor T. McBride

"On the sea"
Artist: Blake Davis
Photo courtesy US Navy
Photographer: Mass Comm. Spc. 2nd Class
Nathan A. Bailey

"Praying for me"
Artist: Elizabeth Moug
Photo courtesy iStock

"In foxholes"
Artist: Chris Holquist
Photo courtesy Flora Public Library
Photographer: Cpl. Charles Overstreet

"My buddy lost his life"
Artist: Saul Rip Hansen
Photo courtesy US Army
Photographer: Joe Barrentine

"The perils of war in my memory remain"
Artist: Elizabeth Moug
Photo courtesy iStock
Photographer: Steven Frame Photography

"I came home a man"
Artist: Elizabeth Moug
Photo courtesy Pixabay.com (public domain)

"There are thousands like me"
Artist: Saul Rip Hansen
Photo courtesy 123RF
Photographer: Brenda Kean

"White crosses in row"
Artist: Saul Rip Hansen
Photo courtesy 123RF
Photographer: Jordi Clave Garsot

"Names carved"
Artist: Saul Rip Hansen
Photo courtesy Alamy Stock Photo
Photographer: Eyal Nahmias

"I'm part of a fellowship"
Artist: Brittany Gneiting
Photo courtesy US Air Force
Photographer: Senior Airman Nathanael Callon

"A strong, mighty band"
Artist: Brian Astle
Photo courtesy US Navy
Photographer: Petty Officer 2nd Class Christopher Menzie

"Each man and each woman"
Artist: Elizabeth Moug
Photo courtesy US Army
Photographer: Justin Connaher

"When old glory waves"
Artist: Brian Astle
Photo courtesy US Air Force
Photographer: Airman 1st Class Tenley Long

"Folded Flag"
Artist: Elizabeth Moug
Photo courtesy St. Louis Honor Flight
Photographer: Bob Vogt

"I am a veteran"
Artist: Elizabeth Moug
Photo courtesy White House photographer David Bohrer

"I am a veteran-collage"
Artist: Brian Astle
Photo collage courtesy Andrea C. Brett

To learn more about this book & the I Am a Veteran Project,

please visit iamaveteran.net.